NATURAL FOOD THERAPY

www.naturalfoodtherapy.co.uk

Contents

One of the biggest challenges for people trying to eat healthily is snacking. It is often considered as unhealthy and a guilty pleasure, however snacking does not have to be unhealthy at all. In this book you will find a collection of nutritionally balanced snack recipes, that are rich in nutrients and will naturally help to support your energy levels, weight, gut health, mood and overall well-being.

Snack recipe benefits:

NUTRITIONALLY BALANCED
Nutritionally balanced snack recipes, high in protein and fibre.

RICH IN VITAMINS & MINERALS
Recipes created with healthy ingredients that are naturally rich in vitamins and minerals.

NUTRITIONAL INFORMATION & PORTION GUIDE
Nutritional information and recommended portion sizes included to make it easy for you to know how many servings each batch of snacks will make.

QUICK, EASY & COST-EFFECTIVE
Based on natural ingredients and minimal steps, recipes are designed to be quick, simple and convenient.

100% PLANT-BASED
Working on the principle that many of us could benefit from eating more plant-based food, each recipe has been solely created with plant-based ingredients.

FREE FROM GLUTEN, DAIRY & REFINED SUGAR
All recipes are free from gluten, dairy and refined sugar.

What you'll need:

To create the recipes in this book, useful kitchen items include:

A food processor
A set of cup measures and spoons
Weighing scales
Square and round baking tins
Greaseproof paper
Small and large bowls

STORE CUPBOARD ESSENTIALS:

Keep your store cupboard well stocked with basic ingredients so you'll always have key snack recipe ingredients to hand. It may look like a lot to start with, but once you have them, these ingredients will last for many batches of snacks:

FLOUR, POWDERS & GRAINS
Coconut flour
Chickpea flour
Cocoa powder
Raw cacao powder
Nutritional yeast
Ground almonds
Vanilla protein powder
Gluten free rolled oats

NUTS
Pecan nuts
Cashew nuts
Pine nuts
Hazelnuts

SEEDS
Ground flaxseeds
Shelled hemp seeds
Pumpkin seeds
Sesame seeds

NUT & SEED BUTTERS
Peanut butter
Cashew butter
Almond butter
Sunflower seed butter
Tahini

LEGUMES
Tinned chickpeas

COCONUT-BASED
Coconut oil
Unsweetened desiccated coconut
Coconut sugar

NATURAL SWEETENERS
Maple syrup
Honey
Dates
Apple puree

CHOCOLATE
Dark chocolate (70% cocoa)
Dark chocolate chips

GROUND SPICES
Ceylon cinnamon
Ginger
Allspice
Nutmeg
Chilli powder

OTHER INGREDIENTS
Vanilla extract
Baking powder
Bicarbonate of soda
Sea Salt

A note about balance:

Healthy eating is all about balance. This book includes healthy snacks to enjoy every day, along with naturally delicious treats to enjoy more moderately. In order for you to make informed choices, the nutritional content for each recipe has been calculated and included on each recipe page.

Healthy
Snacking

PER PORTION
210 **KCALS**
6g **CARBS**
8g **PROTEIN**
17g **FAT**
3g **FIBRE**

Coconut & Hemp Seed Bars

These low carb bars are packed full of heart-healthy fats, protein and minerals. An energising and delicious snack, prepared in five simple steps.

MAKES 6 PORTIONS

1 tbsp coconut oil

1 tbsp pumpkin seeds

1 tbsp sesame seeds

2 tbsp unsweetened
  desiccated coconut

6 tbsp shelled hemp seeds

1 tbsp ground flaxseeds

3 tbsp tahini

2 tbsp honey

1 tsp cinnamon

2 tbsp coconut flour

1. Melt the coconut oil in a saucepan over a gentle heat.

2. With the exception of the coconut flour, add the remaining ingredients into a large bowl, then pour in the melted coconut oil and mix together.

3. Stir in the coconut flour until well-combined.

4. Spoon the mixture into a square baking tin. Press into the corners with the back of a spoon so that the mixture is flat.

5. Refrigerate the bars for at least an hour. Once chilled, slice into 6 bars.

PER PORTION
194 **KCALS**
16g **CARBS**
10g **PROTEIN**
10g **FAT**
2g **FIBRE**

50g dark chocolate
(70% cocoa solids)
350g silken tofu
2 tbsp maple syrup
1 tbsp cocoa powder

Chocolate Mousse

A guilt-free way to get your ultimate chocolate fix. This recipe is naturally rich in protein, requiring just four ingredients and a quick whizz in the blender!

MAKES 3 PORTIONS

1. Melt the chocolate in a heatproof bowl over a pan of barely simmering water (don't let the water touch the bowl or it may burn the chocolate).

2. Once the chocolate has melted, add it to a food processor along with the remaining ingredients.

3. Blend until smooth.

4. Refrigerate the mousse for a minimum of 2 hours.

Chocolate Orange Mousse

To create a chocolate orange version of this recipe, add the juice and zest of one orange along with one extra tablespoon of cocoa powder to the food processor at step 2 of the recipe.

230 **KCALS** | 21g **CARBS** | 11g **PROTEIN** | 11g **FAT** | 3g **FIBRE**

1 cup gluten free
    rolled oats
⅓ cup ground pecans
1 tsp cinnamon
1 pinch sea salt
⅓ cup tahini
¼ cup maple syrup

Maple Tahini Cookies

Maple and tahini are a match made in heaven! Try this naturally-sweetened cookie recipe packed with oats, nuts and seeds.

MAKES 6 PORTIONS (EACH PORTION IS 2 COOKIES)

1. Using a large bowl, mix together the oats, pecans, cinnamon and salt.

2. Pour in the tahini and maple syrup, mixing until well-combined.

3. Allow the mixture to rest for 15 minutes on the side, whilst you preheat the oven to 180°C / 350°F/ gas 4.

4. Once the mixture has rested, roll into 12 balls.

5. Line a baking tin with greaseproof paper and place the balls into the tin. Flatten the balls slightly with the palm of your hand so that they resemble small thick disks.

6. Bake for 12-15 minutes. The cookies will appear under-baked on the baking sheet but will set as they cool.

Peanut Butter Chocolate Chip Blondies

Blondies or 'blonde brownies' are similar to classic chocolate brownies but with a vanilla twist. These blondies contain a secretly healthy ingredient.

MAKES 8 PORTIONS

PER PORTION
194 **KCALS**
19g **CARBS**
7g **PROTEIN**
10g **FAT**
3g **FIBRE**

1½ cups tinned chickpeas, rinsed and drained
½ cup peanut butter
⅓ cup maple syrup
2 tsp vanilla extract
Pinch of sea salt
1 tsp baking powder
⅓ cup dark chocolate chips

1. Preheat the oven to 180°C/ 350°F/ gas 4 and line a 20 x 20cm baking tin with greaseproof paper.

2. Add all of the ingredients apart from the chocolate chips to a food processor and blend until smooth.

3. Fold in two-thirds of the chocolate chips.

4. Spread the mixture evenly into the prepared baking tin and sprinkle the remaining chocolate chips on top.

5. Bake in the oven for 25-30 minutes until lightly golden on the surface. The blondies will appear under-baked on the baking sheet but will firm up as they cool.

6. Allow to cool for 20-30 minutes and then slice into 8 bars.

PER PORTION
165 **KCALS**
15g **CARBS**
6g **PROTEIN**
9g **FAT**
3g **FIBRE**

Gingerbread Blondies

These gingerbread blondies are delicately flavoured with sweet spices. Ginger is a powerful superfood that has been used medicinally for centuries to soothe the digestive tract, reduce inflammation and ease painful joints.

MAKES 8 PORTIONS

1½ cups tinned chickpeas,
   rinsed and drained
½ cup almond butter
⅓ cup maple syrup
1 tsp vanilla extract
2 tsp ground ginger
1 tsp ground cinnamon
Pinch each of allspice,
   nutmeg & sea salt
1 tsp baking powder
¼ tsp bicarbonate of soda
2 pieces of stem ginger
   in syrup, chopped

1. Preheat the oven to 180°C/ 350°F/ gas 4 and line a 20 x 20cm baking tin with greaseproof paper.

2. Add all of the ingredients apart from the stem ginger to a food processor and blend until smooth.

3. Fold in the chopped stem ginger.

4. Spread the mixture evenly into the prepared baking tin.

5. Bake in the oven for 25-30 minutes until lightly golden on the surface. The blondies will appear under-baked on the baking sheet but will firm up as they cool.

6. Allow to cool for 20-30 minutes and then slice into 8 bars.

Cashew Pecan Blondies

The perfect partner to a mid-afternoon cup of tea, this blondie recipe is flavoured with pecan nuts, cashew nuts and maple syrup. Nuts are a great stress-busting snack, high in vitamins and minerals as well as heart-healthy and brain-supportive fats.

MAKES 10 PORTIONS

1½ cups tinned chickpeas, rinsed and drained
1 cup pecans
⅓ cup cashew butter
⅓ cup maple syrup
2 tsp vanilla
Pinch of salt
1 tsp baking powder

1. Preheat the oven to 180°C/ 350°F/ gas 4 and line a 20 x 20cm baking tin with greaseproof paper.

2. Add all of the ingredients to a food processor and blend until smooth.

3. Spread the mixture evenly into the prepared baking tin.

4. Bake in the oven for 25-30 minutes until lightly golden on the surface. The blondies will appear under-baked on the baking sheet but will firm up as they cool.

5. Allow to cool for 20-30 minutes and then slice into 10 bars.

Spicy Peanut Tempeh Skewers

Tempeh is a fermented soybean product often described as a healthier version of tofu. It is high in protein, fibre, vitamins and minerals. Firm tofu can be used in place of tempeh for this recipe.

MAKES 4 PORTIONS

PER PORTION
190 **KCALS**
7g **CARBS**
15g **PROTEIN**
11g **FAT**
6g **FIBRE**

200g tempeh
1 tsp sesame seeds
3 tbsp smooth
   peanut butter
1 tbsp tamari soy sauce
1 tbsp maple syrup
1 clove of garlic, crushed
¼ tsp chilli powder
Generous squeeze
   of fresh lime
1–2 tbsp water

1. Cut the tempeh into cubes.

2. In a large bowl whisk together the remaining ingredients apart from the sesame seeds, to create a marinade.

3. Add the marinade to the tempeh cubes and mix until the tempeh is evenly coated.

4. Cover with cling film and leave to marinate in the fridge for 30 minutes. Whilst the tempeh is marinating, add 4 wooden skewers to a bowl of water to soak.

5. Preheat the oven to 220°C/ 425°F/ gas 7 and line a baking tray with greaseproof paper.

6. Thread the marinated tempeh onto the soaked wooden skewers and place them on the lined baking tray. Sprinkle the sesame seeds over the top.

7. Bake for 10 minutes, then turn the tempeh skewers over, before baking for a further 5 minutes until starting to crisp.

8. Squeeze fresh lime juice over the top and enjoy the skewers hot or cold.

350g broccoli
1 tbsp ground flaxseeds
    plus 2 tbsp water
60g chickpea flour
3 tbsp nutritional yeast
½ tsp sea salt
1 garlic clove, minced
1 tbsp fresh rosemary,
    chopped
50g dairy free cheddar-
    style cheese, grated

Cheesy Broccoli Bites

Eating broccoli never tasted so good! These delicious cheesy bites count as 1 of your 5 a day and are loaded with plant protein and gut-friendly fibre.

MAKES 4 PORTIONS (EACH PORTION IS 4 BITES)

1. Thoroughly wash the broccoli and cut into florets.

2. Place the broccoli into a steamer basket (or a strainer/colander that fits on top of your saucepan). Set the basket over a pan of boiling water, then cover and steam for 3-5 minutes until the broccoli is tender to the bite.

3. Add the cooked broccoli to a food processor and blend until smooth.

4. In a small bowl, mix the flaxseeds with 2 tablespoons of water and set aside for 5 minutes to thicken.

5. In a separate large bowl, mix the chickpea flour, nutritional yeast, salt, garlic and rosemary together. Then stir in the broccoli, the flaxseed mixture and grated cheese.

6. Divide and shape the broccoli mixture into 16 patties and place onto a baking tin lined with greaseproof paper.

7. Cook in a medium-high grill for 8-10 minutes. Turn the patties over using tongs and grill for a further 6-8 minutes, until lightly brown and starting to crisp.

PER PORTION
222 **KCALS**
15g **CARBS**
10g **PROTEIN**
13g **FAT**
5g **FIBRE**

Pine Nut & Spinach Pancakes

These fluffy pancakes are easy to make and highly nutritious, filled with leafy greens and pine nuts.

MAKES TWO PORTIONS

1 tbsp ground flaxseeds
    plus 2 tbsp water
2 tbsp pine nuts
1½ tbsp ground almonds
1 handful fresh spinach
2 handfuls fresh basil
6 tbsp chickpea flour
2 large garlic cloves
Pinch of salt
2 tsp baking powder
½ cup unsweetened
    almond milk

1. In a small bowl mix the flaxseeds with 2 tablespoons of water and set aside to thicken.

2. In a food processor, blend together all of the remaining ingredients until smooth, then add the flaxseed mixture, pulsing a few times until combined.

3. Place the mixture in the fridge for a minimum of 15 minutes.

4. Heat up a little avocado or olive oil in a pan over a medium heat.

5. When the oil is hot, add a ladle of batter (or two if your frying pan is big enough to cook two pancakes at the same time)

6. Cook the pancakes on one side for a few minutes. Flip the pancakes over and cook for a couple of minutes on the other side before serving.

Carrot Cake Protein Bars

No-bake carrot cake protein bars topped with a vanilla and maple topping. This recipe contains anti-inflammatory spices and uses sunflower seed butter which is rich in protein, healthy fats and vitamin E.

MAKES 6 PORTIONS

PER PORTION
220 **KCALS**
20g **CARBS**
12g **PROTEIN**
10g **FAT**
3g **FIBRE**

For the base:
45g gluten free rolled oats
60g vanilla protein powder
½ tsp cinnamon
A pinch each of nutmeg, all spice & ginger
70g sunflower seed butter
2 tbsp maple syrup
¼ cup unsweetened almond milk
40g grated carrots
45g chopped dates

For the topping:
75g dairy free cream cheese
2 tsp vanilla extract
1½ tbsp maple syrup
2 tsp vanilla protein powder (according to taste)

1. Make the base by blending the oats, protein powder, cinnamon, nutmeg, allspice and ginger in the food processor until it resembles a fine powder.

2. Add the sunflower seed butter, maple syrup and almond milk to the food processor and blend until smooth.

3. Stir in the grated carrots and chopped dates until they are well-combined.

4. Taste and if necessary adjust the sweetness by adding a little more maple syrup.

5. Line a square baking tin with greaseproof paper and spoon in the mixture. Press evenly and firmly with the back of a spoon so that the mixture is flat. Refrigerate whilst making the topping.

6. Whisk all the topping ingredients together in a bowl until you have a smooth mixture without any lumps.

7. Spread over the top of the carrot cake bars and refrigerate for at least 2 hours.

8. Once chilled, slice into 6 bars.

Cookie Dough Protein Balls

These cookie dough balls taste like the real deal, yet are packed with protein and slow-release fuel to keep you going. With nutritional benefits and great flavour in equal measure, these healthy treats are ideal for snacking.

MAKES 6 PORTIONS (EACH PORTION IS 2 BALLS)

PER PORTION
235 **KCALS**
19g **CARBS**
10g **PROTEIN**
13g **FAT**
2g **FIBRE**

70g gluten free rolled oats
60g cashew nuts
30g vanilla protein powder
70g smooth cashew butter
30g maple syrup
25–50ml cashew milk
30g dark chocolate chips

1. Preheat the oven to 180°C/ 350°F/ gas 4 and line a baking tin with greaseproof paper.

2. In a food processor blend the oats and cashew nuts together until they form a powder.

3. Add the protein powder, cashew butter and maple syrup to the food processor and blend until combined.

4. Slowly add the cashew milk to the food processor until the mixture resembles a dough.

5. Stir in the chocolate chips by hand and then roll into 12 balls.

6. Place the balls onto a baking tin lined with greaseproof paper and bake for 5 minutes. Serve warm.

Tropical Green Smoothie

Whizz up this high protein smoothie full of detoxifying and nourishing ingredients.

MAKES 1 PORTION

1 large handful of
   baby spinach
50g celery
125g cucumber
25g avocado
50g frozen pineapple
25g vanilla protein powder
Small handful fresh
   mint leaves
Juice of half a lime
1 cup of water

1. Roughly chop the celery, cucumber and avocado.

2. Put all the ingredients into a blender and pulse a few times, then blend until smooth.

3. Pour the smoothie into a glass to serve.

PER PORTION
125 **KCALS**
15g **CARBS**
5g **PROTEIN**
5g **FAT**
5g **FIBRE**

150g papaya
50g plain dairy-
    free yoghurt
1½cm piece of
    fresh ginger
1 cardamom pod
3 fresh mint leaves
1 cup of unsweetened
    almond milk

Happy Gut Smoothie

*This smoothie is great for soothing the stomach
and is a rich source of vitamin C. It is IBS-friendly,
containing ingredients with anti-inflammatory,
anti-bloat and anti-nausea properties.*

MAKES 1 PORTION

1. Roughly chop the papaya and ginger.

2. Deseed the cardamom pod by crushing the pod
with the flat blade of a knife in order to split it open.
Save the seeds and discard the cardamom pod shells.

3. Add all ingredients together in a blender and pulse
a few times, then blend until smooth.

4. Pour into a glass to serve.

Naturally
delicious
treats

Signature Apple Crumble

My signature apple crumble recipe is a family favourite, with a base of juicy baked apples, topped with a nutty, crunchy crumble. Both nutritious and delicious!

MAKES 8 PORTIONS

6 medium-sized apples
½ cup coconut oil
⅓ cup maple syrup
½ cup chopped
    pecan nuts
½ cup ground almonds
1 cup of gluten-free
    rolled oats
2 tbsp ground flaxseeds
2 tsp ground cinnamon
Pinch of nutmeg, mixed
    spice & sea salt

1. Preheat the oven to 200°C/ 400°F/ gas 6.

2. Peel and core the apples before cutting them into chunks and placing into a baking dish.

3. Sprinkle 1 tsp of the cinnamon onto the apples and bake for 20-25 minutes until the apples start to soften.

4. Whilst the apples are in the oven, begin making the topping by melting the coconut oil over a low heat on the hob.

5. Once the oil has melted, add all the remaining ingredients in a bowl, then stir in the coconut oil.

6. Evenly top the softened apple chunks with the moist oat mixture.

7. Place the dish back in the oven and bake for 25-30 minutes until the crumble topping starts to brown.

8. Allow to cool slightly before serving.

PER PORTION
200 **KCALS**
7g **CARBS**
5g **PROTEIN**
17g **FAT**
1g **FIBRE**

Cashew Butter Fudge

A creamy melt-in-your-mouth freezer fudge made with only three ingredients. Little bites of heaven that can be eaten straight out of the freezer!

MAKES 10 PORTIONS

250g cashew butter
35g coconut oil
2 tbsp maple syrup
Pinch of sea salt

1. Line a square baking tin with greaseproof paper.

2. Place the coconut oil and cashew butter in a heavy-based saucepan. Heat slowly, stirring continuously on a low heat for 2 minutes, just until the coconut oil has dissolved and the cashew butter has melted.

3. Remove from the heat and stir in the maple syrup and salt.

4. Pour the mixture into the tin and place in the freezer for a minimum of 2 hours.

5. Once set, cut the fudge into 10 pieces and serve.

PER PORTION
240 **KCALS**
15g **CARBS**
5g **PROTEIN**
18g **FAT**
3g **FIBRE**

Raw Cacao
& Hazelnut Pie

*This deceivingly nutritious recipe features avocado;
full of nutrients and high in heart-healthy fats as well
as providing a sumptuous creamy texture to the pie.*

MAKES 12 PORTIONS

For the base:

200g roasted hazelnuts,
   chopped
50g cashew nuts
50g dates
1 tsp vanilla extract

For the filling:

200g ripe avocado
20g coconut oil, melted
40g raw cacao powder
2 tsp vanilla extract
Pinch sea salt
1 tsp cinnamon
150g honey

1. Line a 23cm round baking tin with greaseproof paper.

2. For the base, add hazelnuts, cashews, dates and
1 teaspoon of the vanilla extract into a food processor.

3. Blend the mixture for a few minutes until it begins to
come together. If it is very dry, you can add a tablespoon
of water to form a sticky consistency.

4. Press the mixture into the bottom of the tin,
applying even pressure with your hand or a spoon.
Refrigerate for at least 30 minutes.

5. Whilst the base is setting, blend all of the filling
ingredients in a food processor until smooth.

6. Once the base is chilled, take it out of the fridge
and pour the filling over the top. Smooth the filling
with a spatula and place in the fridge for at least
5 hours or overnight to firm up.

200g ripe avocado
60g tinned full fat
   coconut milk
1 tbsp fresh lime juice
100g honey

Avocado Ice Cream

An indulgent, sweet and creamy no-churn ice cream, that makes the perfect summer treat.

MAKES 4 PORTIONS

1. Blend together all ingredients in a food processor until smooth.

2. Freeze for a minimum of 4 hours and serve.

NOTE: If you leave the ice cream in the freezer for longer than 4 hours, take it out of the freezer for at least 30 minutes in order to thaw the ice cream prior to eating.

Dark Chocolate Brownies

PER PORTION
230 **KCALS**
24g **CARBS**
4g **PROTEIN**
13g **FAT**
4g **FIBRE**

Indulgent dark chocolate brownies that are decadent, moist, fudgy and easy to make. This brownie recipe is naturally sweetened with apples and a touch of coconut sugar.

MAKES 6 PORTIONS

45g gluten free rolled oats
150g dark chocolate
    (70% cocoa solids)
200g apple puree*
1 tbsp ground flaxseeds
1 tbsp coconut flour
2 tbsp coconut sugar
1 tsp vanilla extract
1 pinch of sea salt
½ tsp bicarbonate of soda
2 tbsp dark chocolate chips
    plus extra for topping

*Apple puree can be bought or made at home. To make it yourself, simply peel and core apples, cook in a pan until soft, then puree in a food processor.

1. Preheat the oven to 180°C/ 350°F/ gas 4 and line a 20x20cm square baking tin with greaseproof paper.

2. Add the oats to a food processor and blend on a high speed until they resemble a fine powder.

3. Melt the chocolate in a heatproof bowl over a pan of gently simmering water. Once the chocolate has melted, take the bowl off the heat and allow it to cool slightly.

4. In a large bowl mix together the ground oats, apple puree, ground flaxseeds, coconut flour, coconut sugar, vanilla extract, sea salt, bicarbonate of soda and melted chocolate. Lastly stir in the chocolate chips.

5. Spoon the mixture into the baking tin. Press into the corners with the back of a spoon so that the mixture is flat. Sprinkle some extra chocolate chips over the top. Bake in the preheated oven for 35 minutes.

6. Once the brownies are baked, allow them to cool in the tin and then cut into 6 squares to serve.

NATURAL FOOD THERAPY
www.naturalfoodtherapy.co.uk

Recipes by nutritional therapist Sasha Paul
Photography by Magda Tymczyj
Design by Smith & Gilmour
Editing by Nikki Paul

Printed in Great Britain
by Amazon